MAGIC TREE HOUSE®

SURVIVAL GUIDE

Mary Pope Osborne and
Natalie Pope Boyce
illustrated by Sal Murdocca

A STEPPING STONE BOOK™
Random House 🏠 New York

Special thanks to Laurence Gonzales, author of
Deep Survival, *for his help with this book*

Text copyright © 2014 by Mary Pope Osborne and Natalie Pope Boyce
Cover art and new colorized illustrations copyright © 2014
by Sal Murdocca

The illustrations that appear herein were originally published in different
form in various Magic Tree House titles.

Magic Tree House is a registered trademark of Mary Pope Osborne;
used under license.

Visit us on the Web!
SteppingStonesBooks.com
MagicTreeHouse.com

Educators and librarians, for a variety of teaching tools, visit us at
RHTeachersLibrarians.com

Library of Congress Cataloging-in-Publication Data
Osborne, Mary Pope.
Magic tree house survival guide / Mary Pope Osborne and Natalie Pope
Boyce ; illustrated by Sal Murdocca.
p. cm. — (A stepping stone book)
Summary: "Jack and Annie show readers how to survive their many
thrilling adventures." —Provided by publisher.
ISBN 978-0-553-49737-3 (trade) — ISBN 978-0-553-49832-5 (lib. bdg.) —
ISBN 978-0-553-49738-0 (ebook)
1. Survival—Juvenile literature. I. Boyce, Natalie Pope.
II. Murdocca, Sal, illustrator. III. Title.
GF86.O74 2014 613.6'9—dc23 2014000269

MANUFACTURED IN CHINA

10 9 8 7 6 5 4 3 2 1

Contents

We've had some really incredible adventures. Remember when we escaped a buffalo stampede, thanks to White Buffalo Woman? Or the time Morning Breeze saved us from a cobra's deadly venom?

Our most exciting adventures have also been our most dangerous. Of course, we had help from friends like a brave knight, a mouse named Peanut, and even a Spider Queen.

And along the way, we've learned some great survival skills. Here are some of our tips for surviving all kinds of scary situations. Look for special notes from us throughout this book. Chances are you'll never need them, but in case you do, here they are. (Spider Queens don't come along every day!)

Jack Annie

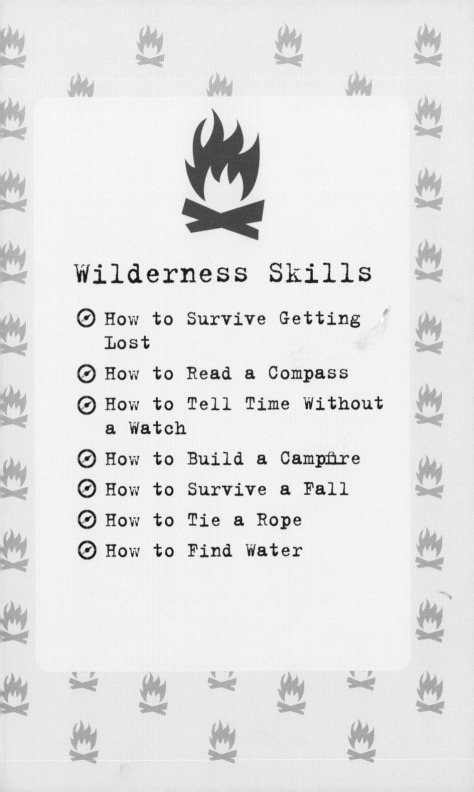

Wilderness Skills

- ⊙ How to Survive Getting Lost
- ⊙ How to Read a Compass
- ⊙ How to Tell Time Without a Watch
- ⊙ How to Build a Campfire
- ⊙ How to Survive a Fall
- ⊙ How to Tie a Rope
- ⊙ How to Find Water

How to Survive

GETTING LOST

Can you imagine getting lost inside a dark Egyptian pyramid or a gigantic Chinese tomb? We actually did! A black cat and a magical ball of thread led us out of those places.

You can't rely on magic if you get lost, but there are some things you can do to help yourself. For one, try not to get lost in the first place! When people get lost, it's usually while they're hiking alone in places they've never been before.

When we hike, we always go with other people. It's safer and a lot more fun. Before we leave home, we put water, snacks, and whistles in our backpacks. Here are some things we've learned about getting lost in the wilderness:

Wilderness Skills

5

1. Sit down and calm down.

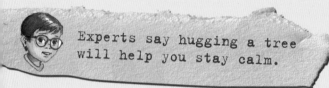

Experts say hugging a tree will help you stay calm.

2. Stay where you are. Don't wander off hoping you will find your way back. Rescuers can find you more easily if you stay put.

3. Make lots of noise. Yell, sing, and call for help. If you have a whistle, blow it three times in a row and then stop for a few minutes before you blow it again. This is a signal that you are in trouble.

4. To make your water last, sip it instead of gulping it. And even if you're hungry, don't eat wild berries or leaves. They might be poisonous.

5. At night, you can build a shelter by

piling branches or leaves on top of one another.

6. During the day, stay out in the open so people in helicopters or airplanes can see you.

7. If you hear a helicopter or plane, stand in a clearing and wave a sweatshirt or whatever else you have to attract attention.

8. Be patient. You can bet that help is on the way!

You'd be safe in this shelter!

How to

READ A COMPASS

The ninjas taught us to use nature as our guide. On our adventures with them, we needed to go east. We put a stick in the ground so that moonlight could shine on it. The shadow of the stick told us which way east was. If you want to know directions, a compass is a lot easier to use than a stick!

There are four main points on a compass: north, south, east, and west. The needle always points north.

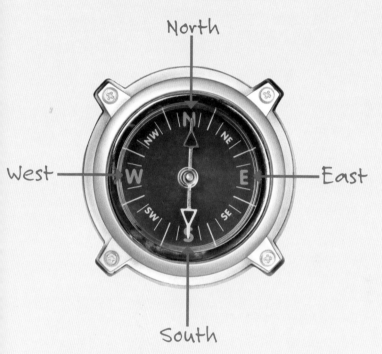

North

West

East

South

Practice by making up directions for yourself. Your plan might look something like this: Using your compass, walk north to the nearest tree. From there, go west until you can touch a house. Now walk south to the nearest car. Finally walk east to another tree.

How to Tell Time

The sun rises in the east and sets in the west. At around nine in the morning, the sun will be halfway between the eastern horizon and its highest point.

When it reaches its highest point, the sun is directly overhead. It's about noon—time for lunch!

Then the sun moves toward the west. Halfway to the western horizon, it's about three o'clock in the afternoon. As the sun sets, evening falls. It's dinnertime!

You can also tell time by looking at a cat's eye! A cat's pupils—the black part of the eye—

10

change to let in more or less light throughout the day. They are usually slits at midday, when the sun is strongest, ovals at midmorning and midafternoon, and round at night.

Must be high noon!

How to
BUILD A CAMPFIRE

Knowing how to start a campfire really comes in handy. You can cook your food, get warm, dry your clothes, and maybe even keep animals and insects away.

First, gather up some dry pieces of wood. It's really hard to burn wet wood. Then search for dried leaves or moss to use as tinder and small

Lip balm is often made out of petroleum. If you have some with you, burning it will help the kindling catch fire.

sticks to use for kindling. These things catch fire quickly and help the larger pieces of wood to burn.

Find a clearing away from piles of leaves, bushes, or trees. Lay down some dry wood and then pile leaves on top. Pile the small sticks onto the leaves and finish up with the larger pieces of wood on the very top.

With an adult's help, use matches to light the tinder. (Don't forget to strike the match away from you, or you might become a campfire yourself!) Once the fire starts, cook some good food, stay warm, and sing campfire songs until you get tired.

How to

SURVIVE A FALL

In Egypt we went rock climbing to save a baby baboon. Falling down a cliff is no laughing matter. Knowing how to fall is a skill that everyone can learn.

It sounds crazy, but a few people have even fallen from airplanes and lived. Just don't try to be one of them!

1. If you fall down a cliff or off a ledge, grab anything you can, like branches, big rocks, or other ledges. This will slow the speed of your fall, and you won't hit as hard when you land.

Vesna Vulović holds the world record for surviving a fall from the greatest height—33,330 feet!

2. Try to relax while you're falling. If your muscles are tense, your injuries will be more serious. Keeping your knees slightly bent will also help.

3. Cover your head, and try to land on your feet.

4. As you drop toward the ground, point your toes and hold your legs together so that you land on the ground on the balls of your feet with both feet hitting at the same time.

5. When you hit the ground, you'll bounce, so fall the way paratroopers do and roll to your left or right side. It's called a PLF, or a parachute landing fall.

How to

TIE A ROPE

Mountain and rock climbers link themselves together with ropes. If one of them slips, the ropes are a secure way to keep from falling. Tying a good knot is a skill anyone can master. One of the best knots is the square knot.

A square knot links two ropes together. Sailors have used it for centuries, and mountain climbers and farmers use it, too.

1. Hold the end of one rope over another.

2. Cross the left end of one rope over and under the right end of the other.

3. Cross the right end over and under the left end.

4. Hold both ends together and pull to tighten the knot.

To remember how to tie a square knot, memorize this saying: right over left and under; left over right and under. Try to sing it—singing is a good way to remember just about anything!

How to

FIND WATER

If you're in the wilderness, remember that you need water every single day. Streams, creeks, and rivers are all good water sources. If none of them are nearby, check holes and cracks in rocks or tree stumps for rainwater.

Water also collects in low-lying areas like ditches and valleys. Just remember that even if the water looks clean, it often carries germs. Many people take water-purifying pills with them when they hike.

Rainwater is the safest drinking water. If it's raining, collect it in pots or on a waterproof sheet or jacket.

Watch where insects and birds are landing, or look for animal tracks. These signs can mean a water source is nearby.

Check out muddy patches of ground. Dig

about a foot down, and it's possible that water will seep into the hole. After putting it in a container, strain the water through a shirt or cloth to get rid of the mud.

There is often dew on the grass in the early morning. Wipe your T-shirt along the grass and squeeze the water into your mouth. Also check plants to see if there is water on their leaves.

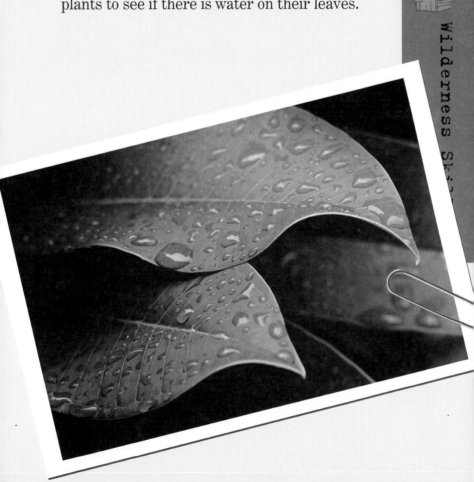

Lions and Tigers and Bears—Oh, Man!

- ⊘ How to Survive a Lion Encounter
- ⊘ How to Survive a Tiger Encounter
- ⊘ How to Survive a Bear Encounter
- ⊘ How to Survive a Stampede
- ⊘ How to Survive a Cobra Bite
- ⊘ How to Survive a Gator Encounter
- ⊘ How to Train a Horse
- ⊘ How to Survive an Octopus Encounter
- ⊘ How to Survive a Shark Encounter
- ⊘ How to Survive a Gorilla Encounter

How to Survive a

LION ENCOUNTER

In Africa, we learned a lot about lions. If a lion lashed its tail back and forth and stared at us, we knew it meant business! (And that business was probably us!) We've never met any other kids who have faced a lion. But here's what we advise if it happens:

1. When a lion stalks you, stand tall, lift your arms above your head, and yell with all your might.

2. If the lion charges, don't run or turn your back. Chances are it's faking an attack. Lions charge at about fifty miles per hour and roar their heads off. Don't move a muscle or even blink your eyes!

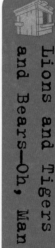

25

3. If the lion backs off, you back off, too . . . very slowly. If the lion starts to move toward you again, freeze once more.

4. Actually it's probably a good idea to stay away from lions on the loose whether they're lashing their tails or not!

Lions in the wild sleep about twenty hours a day.

A group of lions is called a pride.

27

How to Survive a

TIGER ENCOUNTER

Tigers live in India, China, and other parts of Asia. Once we saved a tiger from a poacher's trap. Since they're an endangered species, saving one is a big deal.

Teddy's bark protected us from a tiger, but if you live in a faraway jungle with tigers on the prowl, you'll need a better plan to face the largest cat on earth. Don't worry too much about this happening. You have a better chance of being hit by a meteorite than meeting a tiger that's taking a stroll.

1. If the tiger is far off, run away fast! If it is close by, stand still so it won't see you moving.

2. If you sense that a tiger is behind you, turn around and yell, roar, scream, snarl, bark, hoot, and shout! Hold up your arms and wave them so that you look tall. Walk like a zombie! Like all cats, even house cats, tigers like to ambush their prey and usually attack from behind. Your actions might scare it away.

3. Grab the biggest rock or stick you can find. Act fierce and brave, and hit it with all you've got! Tigers don't usually expect much of a fight. Bold action on your part might give you a chance to escape. Good luck! (You'll need it.)

Since tigers attack from behind, people have found they are much safer wearing masks on the backs of their heads.

How to Survive a

BEAR ENCOUNTER

Remember in the Arctic, when a polar bear saved our lives? Your chances of meeting a polar bear are very small. They live way up north in the Arctic Circle. But if you ever do come across a polar bear, or any other kind of bear, you shouldn't expect it to save you. It will probably think of you as a very tasty breakfast! Here's what to do if you meet a bear:

1. Always walk in a group when you're in bear country. Make a lot of noise. Sing, yell, or clap your hands! Bears need some warning that you're around.

2. If a bear appears, don't look it in the eye. Back away from it very slowly.

33

3. Trees are no help. Bears can climb. Running is no good. Bears run way faster than you can.

4. Bears with cubs are especially likely to be aggressive. If a bear charges, drop down and curl up into a ball on your stomach. Protect the back of your neck with your hands or backpack.

5. Play dead, and don't make a peep. The bear may lose interest. If it walks away, lie still for a while. Then get up and move away slowly.

6. Never leave food out when you're camping. Keep it in a bear-proof container. Bears have a great sense of smell, so ordinary containers won't work.

7. If a bear attacks you while you're in a tent, grab whatever you can find and try to hit the bear hard in the nose or eyes.

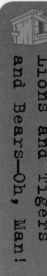

How to Survive a

STAMPEDE

Stampedes are scary! Unless you and your friends are in a rush to get out to recess, you'll probably never know what it's like to be in a stampede. We survived one with the help of White Buffalo Woman.

When animals like bison or cattle stampede, they don't care who or what they run over. So if you're planning to be a cowboy and work around cattle, this advice is for you!

Lions and
and Bears—

1. Anything from a soft noise to the sudden movement of a horse or person can spook cattle and make them stampede. This is especially true at night.

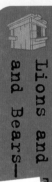

2. Move your horse away from the herd if you need to jump off.

3. Cowboys sing to their cattle to keep them calm. You might try that if you want to prevent a stampede. Just don't sing anything too wild.

4. Cattle don't like to turn left. With this in mind, cowboys ride ahead of stampeding cattle and turn them to the right until they begin to run in a tight circle. When the circle gets too tight, the cattle will begin to slow down and stop.

5. If you are off your horse during a stampede, try getting to the nearest tree, rock, or whatever you can find. Singing won't help you at all.

How to Survive a

COBRA BITE

There are many different kinds of cobras, but you'll probably never meet one unless you're at the zoo. On our adventure in India, we had to get an emerald from right under a king cobra's watchful eyes. And we were only six inches tall. Seriously.

When cobras strike, they hiss, flatten the hoods on their necks, and raise their heads off the ground. Their hissing sounds like a low growl. But the scariest thing about them is their venom, which is often deadly.

1. It's a good idea to take antivenin with you if you're going to an area where there are cobras.

2. If you are unlucky enough to get a cobra bite, try to stay calm. (Yeah, right!) Fear makes your heart

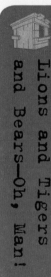

Lions and Tigers and Bears—Oh, Man!

41

beat faster and makes the venom spread rapidly through your body.

3. You need to get help immediately! Head for the nearest hospital! Even if you have antivenin, you need to see a doctor.

Or maybe you should make friends with a mongoose!

How to Survive a

GATOR ENCOUNTER

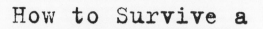

When we were on the Amazon, Annie thought she was grabbing a branch, but it was really a crocodile! We learned that crocodiles and alligators live in the tropics both on land and in water. When they're in the water, they look just like floating logs.

The next time we're in gator country, we won't dangle our hands over the sides of a boat. And we'll always be really careful at night, when gators are most active. Here are some things you should know about crocs and gators:

1. Walk carefully, and be alert. These animals can remain still for hours and are often hard to spot.

2. Mother gators and crocs will attack in a heartbeat if they are protecting their eggs or babies, so watch for signs of a nest.

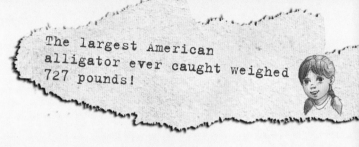

The largest American alligator ever caught weighed 727 pounds!

3. Back away if a gator takes an interest in you. They attack suddenly, so don't get close.

4. If one attacks, hit it on the nose with anything you can find! This will make it open its mouth, and you might be able to escape.

5. Never feed these animals. It makes them more likely to approach people if they think they can easily get food.

How to

TRAIN A HORSE

When we met Alexander the Great's magnificent stallion, Bucephalus, he was wild. We tried to ride him, but he bolted! Alexander didn't use force to train Bucephalus. Instead, he realized that the horse was afraid of his own shadow and turned him away from the sun before mounting him. Then he spoke gently to him before riding him. Here are some great tips for training a horse:

1. Spend time getting to know the horse when it's in the stall. Talk gently to it, pat it, and groom it whenever you can. Visit it a lot until it gets used to seeing you.

2. Try putting on a halter that has a long rope attached to it. Lead the

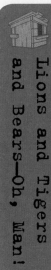

Lions and Tigers and Bears—Oh, Man!

47

horse outside and walk it around you in a large circle.

3. Using the rope as a guide, work with the horse to teach it voice commands like "walk," "trot," and "stop."

4. Put a bridle and saddle on the horse. Let it move around until it feels comfortable wearing them.

5. Mount the horse from the left and press its sides with your knees to coax it into a walk.

6. Ride your horse and work with it often until it walks, trots, canters, and gallops at your command.

7. Don't expect to train a horse in just one day or even one week. If you love your horse and take good care of it, you'll have a friend for life!

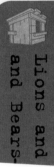

How to Survive an

OCTOPUS ENCOUNTER

We've met giant octopuses twice. On our deep-sea adventure, a giant octopus saved us. At first, we thought it was going to strangle us and pull us under the ocean. But when we relaxed, we realized it was trying to save us from drowning. We found out that these creatures are shy and very smart. They only attack when they are scared.

Octopuses don't squeeze you to death. They are usually not dangerous to humans. One type that people need to watch out for is the blue-ringed octopus. It has a very venomous bite. The blue-ringed octopus sleeps during the day and is active at night. It is a little over five inches long and lives around coral reefs from Japan to Australia.

1. If you come across any kind of octopus, don't try to touch it.

51

2. Some will send out an inky liquid that hides them and allows them to escape. This gives you a chance to back off as well.

3. The blue-ringed octopus doesn't do this. Instead, its blue rings begin to glow and shimmer! They are warnings to stay away.

4. Keep in mind that the blue-ringed octopus is shy, and very few people have ever died from its bite.

A blue-ringed octopus in Indonesia

How to Survive a

SHARK ENCOUNTER

Imagine you're at the beach and someone screams, "Shark!" People will leap out of the water in half a second! Nothing scares people more than a shark sighting. But you are more likely to be hit on the head with a coconut than to be attacked by a shark. You should have fun at the beach. Just don't stand under a coconut tree!

It helps to know that not all sharks are dangerous. There are more than 400 different kinds, and most are no threat at all.

When we were chased by a shark, two dolphins helped us. But dolphins might not always be around, so it's good to have some information:

1. Don't swim after dark. Sharks most often feed at night.

2. Never swim where people are fishing. The blood from bait or dead fish is a shark magnet.

3. If you have a cut, don't go in the water. Sharks can smell a single drop of blood without any problem at all.

4. If you see a shark, swim to the shore as smoothly as you can. Don't kick, scream, and splash around. Sharks go after wounded prey, so don't act like one.

5. If a shark gets close enough to attack, punch it hard over and over again in its eyes or gills. These are its weakest spots.

6. Sharks often bump people before attacking. If this happens, swim away as calmly as possible and go back to shore. And then warn everyone by screaming your head off!

7. Now you can ask for an ice cream cone. You deserve one. Actually, maybe two.

How to Survive a

GORILLA ENCOUNTER

We traveled to an African cloud forest and met some fantastic mountain gorillas. The giant male gorilla with silver fur didn't exactly become our immediate best friend. But a little time and a little knowledge helped us all get along. Here's what we learned:

1. Gorillas are shy. They eat plants, not people. However, they have been known to react to people if they feel threatened.

2. If you alarm a gorilla, it will roar, throw sticks, pound its chest, and charge toward you. Most of the time, the gorilla is just faking.

3. Crouch down and keep your eyes on the ground. This tells the gorilla that you mean no harm and that it's the boss! This is the way gorillas treat each other. Bottom line: you play nice, and they will, too.

Beware of this gorilla.

Maybe not this one!

Extreme Weather

How to Survive

EXTREME HEAT

Some places can be really hot in the summer and reach temperatures of over 100 degrees. Very hot weather can raise your body temperature. High temperatures often cause people to sweat and lose the water their bodies need. This is called dehydration.

Dehydration puts you in danger of a heat stroke. Heat strokes can be deadly! When we went back in time to the Civil War, we helped a drummer boy who was weak from heat stroke.

In very hot weather, we dress in light clothes that reflect heat away from our bodies, and we always wear hats. We drink a lot of water, especially when we exercise. It's smart to drink more than you think you need.

61

We never exercise outside during the hottest time of the day. We know the signs of heat stroke—dizziness, hot red skin, and no sweating. If we ever felt those symptoms, we'd head for a cool place right away and tell an adult. Not preparing for super-hot weather is not cool!

Water sports are perfect for a hot summer day!

How to Dress for

EXTREME COLD

Oh, brother! When we were in the Arctic, the Antarctic, and the freezing kingdom of the Ice Wizard, we found out what being cold really means! But the coldest we've ever been was when we climbed into the magic tree house in our bathing suits and shorts and went back in time to the Ice Age. Brrrr!

Wearing the right clothes in the cold is very important. When we have time to plan, here's how we dress for very cold temperatures:

1. We always wear several layers of clothes under a waterproof coat or jacket.
2. We make sure that our clothes are clean and not muddy or wet when we put them on. Clean, dry clothes hold in the heat best.
3. We always put on warm hats, mittens, boots, thick socks, and scarves. Experts say that mittens are warmer than gloves. Your boots shouldn't be too tight. You should dry them out every night so they aren't wet the next day.

Shivering is a way for your body to make heat. It's also a sign that you are too cold. Go inside and get some hot chocolate!

If your skin turns pale and becomes numb, frostbite is a real possibility. Head home right away and get an adult to check you out.

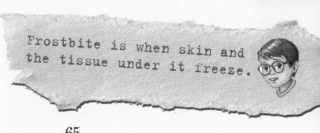

Frostbite is when skin and the tissue under it freeze.

65

How to Survive a

SANDSTORM

Remember when we were in a sandstorm in the Middle East? Blowing sand feels like little bits of stinging rock when it hits your skin. We couldn't breathe well, and we couldn't see very far, either.

A sandstorm can come up in seconds. A huge dark cloud of dust and debris will suddenly sweep across the land, blotting out the sun. Here's what you can do to survive:

1. Branches and all kinds of things will sail through the air and could hurt you. If you are in a car, tell whoever is driving to pull off the road. Stay in the car!

2. If you're outside and in a group, stay together. If possible, try to get to higher ground. Most blowing sand stays lower down.

3. If you can't find shelter, look for a boulder or other large object to crouch behind. If there's nothing nearby, lie down to avoid being hit with flying objects.

4. Protect your eyes, nose, and mouth with anything you have, like a backpack or sweatshirt. We protected our faces with cloths. You can also use your hands.

How to Survive a

TWISTER

We know firsthand how scary a tornado, or twister, can be. We were on the Kansas prairie when the sky turned a strange greenish color. Then a funnel-shaped cloud appeared on the horizon. Tornadoes can flatten whole towns and toss cars around like toys, but there are ways to prepare for and survive these terrible storms.

Extreme Weather

1. Twisters form out of thunder-storms. It's a good idea to check for tornado warnings whenever there's a big thunderstorm.
2. Check to see if the clouds are low and moving quickly. Also look at the color of the sky. A sickly green or yellow sky is a danger sign.
3. Go down to the basement. If you don't have a basement, head for the first floor and get into a closet or a bathroom without a window. If you're in a bathroom, get into the tub.
4. If you can't do that, get under a sturdy table or desk. Pull a mattress over your body or pile up pillows to protect yourself from flying glass or debris.
5. If you're outside with no shelter, lie down in a ditch and cover your head and neck with your arms.

6. If you're in a car, get out and head for the nearest ditch. Twisters can toss cars into the air.

Remember, you can't run faster than a tornado. People say that their roar sounds like a huge jet engine. It's a sound no one ever forgets!

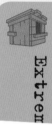

Extrem

How to Stay Safe in a

Thunder and lightning go together. Lightning is electricity that comes from thunderstorms.

If you hear thunder and see flashes of lightning, stay away from the windows. Forget about your TV, computers, or anything else that uses electricity. Lightning may hit the outside lines that lead into your house.

Water conducts electricity, so don't wash your hands or take a shower. If you're swimming, get out of the water fast and take shelter. But be careful where the shelter is. Metal is also a good conductor of electricity. So don't stand under metal sheds, roofs, or bleachers.

Also stay away from trees. A good rule is to check out how tall the nearest tree is and to stay twice that far away from it.

Head to an open area and crouch down. Keep

your feet together, and put your hands over your ears to protect them from the noise.

Even though lightning bolts are only an inch wide, each year they injure and kill more people than lions, cobras, and tigers!

How to Survive a

FLOOD

When we were visiting Venice for Carnival, we learned that the city is actually 118 islands, joined by bridges and canals. At times, high tides from the Adriatic Sea flood the city and threaten its beautiful buildings.

Floods occur when so much rain falls that rivers, creeks, and streams can't hold all the water.

When it's been raining hard for hours or days, check for a flood watch or warning. A flood watch means that a flood is possible. A flood warning means that a flood is on its way or is happening right now.

1. Think about a safe place to go if you have to leave home. It could

be a motel or a shelter or a friend's house on safe, high ground.

2. Try to put as much as you can on the second floor, if you have one. Pack bags with things you'll need, like clothes and medicines.

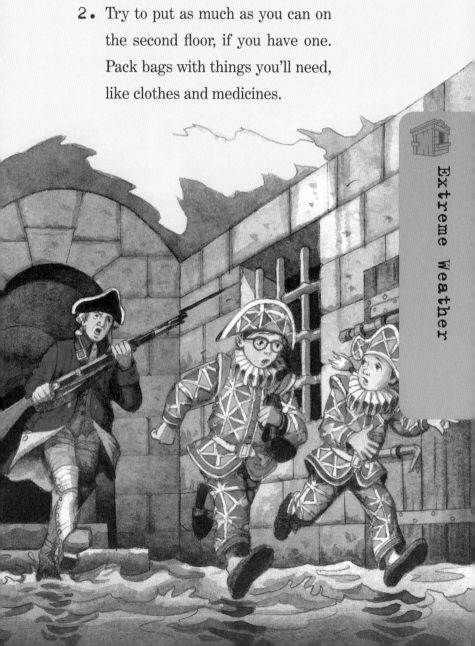

3. If the warning says to leave home right away, do it! Flash floods do come in a flash!
4. Head away from rivers and streams and up to high ground.
5. Don't get out of the car and walk through floodwaters or go around roadblocks. Six inches of rushing water has enough force to knock you down!

How to Prepare for a

POWER OUTAGE

After a big thunderstorm or a natural disaster like a hurricane, twister, or earthquake, the power may go out. There will be no lights, air-conditioning, heat, TV, or radio. If the outage lasts awhile, there might not even be any water. The food in the refrigerator will spoil after several hours. Help!

77

When you hear storm warnings, make sure there are flashlights and candles around the house. Fill the bathtub with water for flushing the toilets. It's also a good idea to stock up on bottled water and canned or packaged food that doesn't need cooking.

If the power goes out at night, grab a good book, turn on your flashlight (leave the candles for the adults), hide under the covers, and read, read, read!

How to Use Nature to

TELL THE WEATHER

TEMPERATURE

Listen to the crickets! Count the number of cricket chirps in fourteen seconds. Then add forty to that number. For example, if you count ten chirps in fourteen seconds, that means it's about fifty degrees Fahrenheit.

DISTANCE OF A THUNDERSTORM

Look for a flash of lightning. Listen for a clap of thunder. Count the seconds between them and divide by five. For example: *Flash!* (Lightning!) *Boom!* (Thunder!) Say you've counted ten seconds in between. Dividing ten by five tells you that the storm is about two miles away. Go inside!

PREDICTING RAIN

Here's a good poem that is usually true:

Red sky at night,
sailors delight.
Red sky in morning,
sailors take warning.

This means that if the sky is red at night, it'll be mild weather. If the sky is red in the morning, it'll probably rain.

Disasters

How to Survive an

EARTHQUAKE

We were in San Francisco when the city suffered a terrible earthquake. The ground started shaking and rumbling. Buildings tumbled down. Fires burned for three days.

Places like Japan, China, and Indonesia have a lot of earthquakes. Here are some tips on how to survive one:

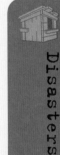

1. If you're inside, remember to duck and cover. Get under a table or a desk. You might also stand in a doorway near the center of the house, as far as possible from the outer walls.

2. Stay away from windows and large pieces of furniture. Windows might shatter, and the furniture could fall. Avoid elevators and stairs, too.

3. If the earthquake happens at night, roll down onto the floor by your bed and put a pillow or blankets over your head.

4. If you are outside, try to get to an open space. Avoid being close to buildings, trees, or power lines.

5. When the shaking stops, wait at least fifteen minutes before you move. If you go outside, watch

out for power lines lying on the ground.

6. After an earthquake, there are usually aftershocks. For a few days, be prepared for more shaking, and continue to follow the rules!

A door is all that remained of this building after an earthquake in India.

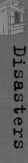

How to Survive a

TSUNAMI

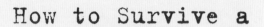

We were amazed at the beauty of Hawaii. But then we saw a giant wave approaching! Hawaii and many countries around the Pacific Ocean have tsunamis caused by earthquakes or volcanoes erupting under the ocean.

A tsunami comes in at high speed as a huge wall of water. The water covers everything in its path. Then it draws far back to sea, pulling everything with it.

When people hear tsunami warning sirens, they get to high ground. But even if there are no sirens, there are things that can warn you. Tilly Smith, a schoolgirl who visited Thailand during a terrible tsunami, saved many lives because she knew what the ocean looks like before a tsunami.

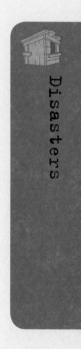

Tilly Smith

1. Tilly saw the ocean bubbling and swirling as she walked along the beach.

2. She also noticed that the tide pulled far back out to sea and rushed in higher than it had been just a few minutes before.

3. In school, Tilly had learned that these were signs of a tsunami. She and her parents alerted everyone to get off the beach.

4. The behavior of animals is another clue. They seem to sense the danger and run from the beach, even before there are any other warning signs. So if you see elephants, dogs, cats, monkeys, rats, mice, or other animals heading for the hills, you'd better join the race, too.

How to Survive a

VOLCANO ERUPTION

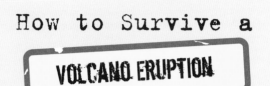

We survived the eruption of Mount Vesuvius by putting pillows over our heads. We were lucky. We escaped, but many other people didn't.

Afterward, we learned better ways to survive an erupting volcano. Here's what we'd do the next time we saw the top of a mountain exploding and tons of lava pouring down the hills and the sky raining ash. (Yikes!)

1. Stay away from streams and valleys, because of flooding and mudflow. Also, toxic gases can collect there.

2. Put our pets (and ourselves) inside and close the windows and doors.

3. If we had time, we'd grab clothes to cover our arms and legs and protect them from burning ash.

4. Since gases from volcanoes can be deadly, we'd curl up in a ball and cover our mouths and noses.

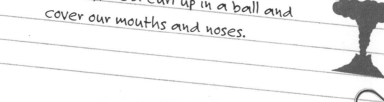

5. Afterward, we would stay away from buildings with a lot of ash on their roofs. They might collapse!

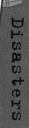

How to Survive an

AVALANCHE

While we were in the Swiss Alps, a huge avalanche came roaring down the mountain and buried us! Saint Bernard dogs trained to find people in deep snow or in avalanches came to our rescue. That's why we're here today! We owe our lives to those brave dogs.

Saint Bernard

Avalanches happen fast. You hear a roar, and before you know it, tons of snow comes thundering down. Avalanches can cover villages, roads, and skiers in minutes.

1. Avalanches are most likely to occur when the weather has been warmer than usual or shortly after a heavy snowfall or storm. Look for warning signs along the trails.

2. If you hear the rumble of an avalanche, let go of your ski poles, backpacks, snowboards, and skis.

3. You can't outrun the wall of snow. Avalanches reach speeds of over eighty miles an hour. The greatest amount of snow is in the middle. If possible, try running to the outer edges.

4. Grab on to anything you can find, like a tree trunk.

5. As the snow begins to cover you, try swimming through it. Use your arms like a swimmer, and kick your legs up toward the surface.

6. After an avalanche covers you, it can be confusing to figure out which way is up. As the snow barrels down, quickly hold one arm over your head so that it points up to the surface.

7. Curl into a ball and turn your head back and forth. This will make a space so you can breathe.

8. Until you can hear rescuers nearby, don't yell. You'll use up valuable oxygen, and the heavy snow will muffle your voice.

9. Try to stay calm until help arrives. There are people and dogs trained as avalanche rescuers. They'll be doing their best to find you.

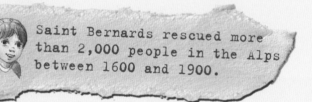

Saint Bernards rescued more than 2,000 people in the Alps between 1600 and 1900.

How to Survive a

FIRE

In Australia, we escaped a scary wildfire. In ancient Japan, we helped put out a huge blaze that would have burned an entire rice harvest.

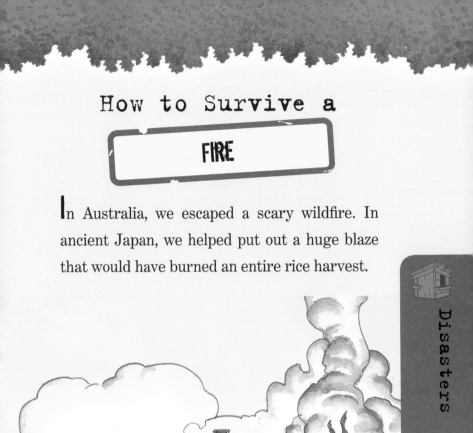

Fires can happen almost anywhere, but most of them occur at home. Tell an adult right away if you ever see sparks coming from an electric cord or appliance. And never, ever play with matches!

Remember to call 911 at the first sign of fire. And remember these important things, too. They could save your life.

1. People are less likely to die from burns than from breathing in smoke.

2. If you hear a smoke alarm go off, leave the building right away. If you smell smoke, do the same thing.

3. If a door feels hot to touch, don't open it. If smoke is coming from under a door but the door isn't hot, use caution and open it a little. Keep your head turned away. Opening the door will feed oxygen to the fire and make it worse.

4. If there is a lot of smoke in the hall, close the door right away and stay inside.

5. Stuff towels, clothes, or anything you can find around the cracks in the door to keep the smoke out.

6. Oxygen is heavier than smoke and stays low to the ground. Crawl along the floor so you can breathe.

7. Firefighters might not be able to see you because of the smoke. If you can, open a window and signal for help by yelling or waving something that is brightly colored.

Incredible Survival

- ⊘ How to Survive a T. Rex Encounter
- ⊘ How to Survive a Pirate Encounter
- ⊘ How to Survive Zero Gravity
- ⊘ How to Survive a Shipwreck
- ⊘ Surviving on Spiders

How to Survive a

T. REX ENCOUNTER

When we traveled back in time to the Cretaceous Period, we had to escape a Tyrannosaurus rex! We took off on the back of a Pteranodon, a huge flying reptile!

Of course, dinosaurs became extinct over 65 million years ago. But that won't stop us from giving you advice in case you come across a Tyrannosaurus rex in your backyard. And what if, like all giant meat-eating dinosaurs, it is super-hungry? Incredible as it sounds, if this ever happens, you might want to have a dinosaur survival plan in mind:

1. Don't believe that the T. rex can't see well. Scientists say that they did. Standing still won't help. It'll just give the T. rex a good laugh. And since a T. rex is over twelve feet tall, hiding behind a bush isn't much help. (Another big laugh for T. rex!)

2. T. rex has fifty to sixty huge teeth, some as long as a banana. It can snap up 500 pounds in the blink of an eye. If you can gain lots of weight, maybe a ton or two in a few minutes, the T. rex will have a hard time gobbling you up. Start eating . . . now! Call in an order for 6,000 pizzas, 4,000 cheeseburgers, and 1,000 chocolate cakes!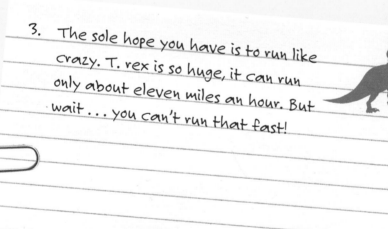

3. The sole hope you have is to run like crazy. T. rex is so huge, it can run only about eleven miles an hour. But wait . . . you can't run that fast!

4. If a T. rex is in your backyard and you hope to survive, stay inside! Call the police! No, that's not enough! Call the president of the United States to send help!

How to Survive a

PIRATE ENCOUNTER

Cap'n Bones, the pirate, was bad news. He locked us up in his pirate ship until we promised to help him find treasure.

If you go back in time 200 years and pirates capture you, here are some good tips on how you can escape:

1. Don't leave home without lemons, limes, or oranges in your pocket. Back then, pirates and other sailors got a disease called scurvy from lack of vitamin C. Scurvy caused them to feel tired and horrible. If you eat the fruit every day, when the pirates get scurvy and are sick in their bunks, you'll be healthy and can escape in a rowboat.

109

2. Pirates say *arrgh* all the time. Every time one says it to you, say "I beg your pardon?" They will get so tired of explaining what *arrgh* means that they'll set you free. (They don't know what it means, either.)

3. If you are captured with your friends, send notes to them with escape plans. Most pirates couldn't read. Your plans will be a secret. And secret plans are the best plans.

4. If the pirates make you walk the plank, go to the end of it, do a perfect swan dive into the ocean, and swim like crazy to the shore.

5. Pirates like to have talking parrots. Make friends with one and

tell it to fly to a friendly ship for help. Teach it to say, "Help! My friends have been kidnapped by pirates! Follow me!" When help arrives, walk proudly off the ship and take the parrot with you.

ARRGH!!

How to Survive

ZERO GRAVITY

If there was no gravity, we'd all float off into space. Gravity is the force that keeps everything on the ground. We had a great journey to the moon and found out what it was like to live with very little gravity.

In low gravity, your body feels as if it weighs much less. If you weigh sixty pounds on earth, you'll weigh ten pounds on the moon.

Pushing off from something makes you bounce around like a ball in slow motion! Your brain keeps on telling you that you're falling, but you never do. Instead, you just float around and feel relaxed all the time.

113

Astronauts in space have to survive with no gravity at all. Washing, eating, and drinking can be a problem. In zero gravity, special containers keep everything from floating away.

When astronauts eat, they attach their food to their trays and need straws to drink. Astronauts also say that they can't smell or taste their food. With no gravity, smells just float away.

Even with all the problems of living with no gravity, it's still a lot of fun. Astronaut Sally Ride said it was the best time she ever had in her life!

If food crumbs got loose, they could mess up the spacecraft's instruments.

How to Survive a

SHIPWRECK

The *Titanic* is probably the most famous shipwreck in history. And we were there! We helped a girl and her little brother get to a lifeboat just before the great ship went down.

Sadly, only 706 of more than 2,200 *Titanic* passengers survived. Today there are rules that make large ships safer. There must be more than enough lifeboats for everyone. And ships steer farther south in winter and spring to avoid icebergs like the one the *Titanic* struck in 1912.

Anytime you get on a boat, there are things you can do to make sure you stay safe:

1. Wear your life jacket! Kids are required to wear life jackets on any private vessel under a certain size. Make sure yours fits snugly and won't slip off in the water.

2. Know where things are on the ship! If you're on a large cruise ship or a ferry, find out where the life jackets and life rafts or lifeboats are stored. Check out

the nearest exits in case you need
to get off the boat quickly.

3. Know your equipment! If your
   boat has an inflatable life raft,
   have an adult help you practice
   inflating it. Many life rafts come
   with emergency items such as
   a first-aid kit, flares, a mirror
   for signaling rescuers, and a
   canopy to protect you from
   the sun and rain. You'll save
   time in an emergency if you know
   what's on hand.

You'll probably never be in a shipwreck. But
if you are, remember these important things:

1. Stay calm. A clear head will help
   you make good choices.
2. If you're not wearing a life jacket,
   put one on right away!
3. If there's time, gather supplies,

especially food and water. Grab blankets, a flashlight, a mirror, and sunscreen.

4. If you have a life raft or lifeboat, get in!

5. If it's light out, use mirrors to signal for help. When it's dark, use a flashlight or flares. But don't use your flares or the batteries in your flashlight until you see or hear possible rescuers. Save them for when you need them most!

6. Protect yourself against heat and cold. Blankets can keep you warm or shade you from the sun. Don't forget about the danger of heat stroke!

7. If you let yourself drift instead of trying to stay in one spot, you have a better chance of reaching land. Then you can use your wilderness skills to survive until help arrives.

Incredible Survival

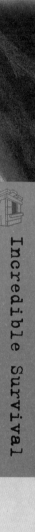

Surviving on

SPIDERS

On our quest for the Sword of Light, we met a Spider Queen. We were really scared of her at first. But when her cave started filling up with water, she saved us by spinning a web ladder so we could escape.

Spiders can be very helpful! They eat pesky insects like mosquitoes. And in one survival story, spiders also helped two men live through a terrible ordeal in the jungle.

In 2007, Loic Pillois and Guilhem Nayral,

from France, got lost in the steamy jungles of French Guiana, which borders Brazil and Suriname. The men had only enough food to last twelve days. They managed to build a shelter and waited to be rescued.

When their food ran out, they began eating insects, turtles, frogs, and—you guessed it—large bird-eating spiders. As they waited, the men were eaten up with insect bites and

parasites. They also faced constant danger from jaguars, snakes, and poison dart frogs.

Trees more than one hundred feet tall blocked their view of the sky. The forest was so thick that no one in a helicopter or plane could find them. In fact, rescuers had given up ever finding them alive.

After three weeks, Loic and Guilhem were desperate. They began walking through marshes and deep jungle underbrush. The men were sick, and rain beat down on them as they trudged through the jungle.

Finally Guilhem got so weak he couldn't keep walking, but Loic managed to reach the village of Saül. A search party quickly set out to rescue his friend.

Four hours later, they came across Guilhem.

Doctors said he would have died in a matter of hours if they hadn't found him. Both men had survived for seven long weeks!

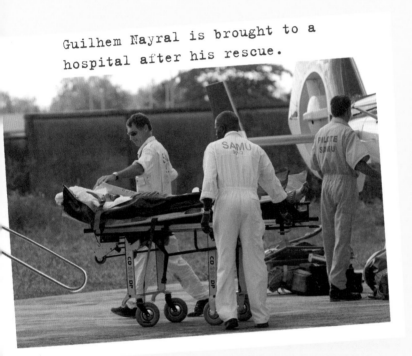

Guilhem Nayral is brought to a hospital after his rescue.

Now that you know how to survive tigers, cobras, blue-ringed octopuses, twisters, a T. rex, pirates, and all kinds of other things, it's time to have a little fun. Maybe you should go outside and build a tree house.

Photograph Credits

Want even more
Magic Tree House fun?

Magic Tree House® Books

Merlin Missions

Magic Tree House® Fact Trackers

DINOSAURS

KNIGHTS AND CASTLES

MUMMIES AND PYRAMIDS

PIRATES

RAIN FORESTS

SPACE

TITANIC

TWISTERS AND OTHER TERRIBLE STORMS

DOLPHINS AND SHARKS

ANCIENT GREECE AND THE OLYMPICS

AMERICAN REVOLUTION

SABERTOOTHS AND THE ICE AGE

PILGRIMS

ANCIENT ROME AND POMPEII

TSUNAMIS AND OTHER NATURAL
DISASTERS

POLAR BEARS AND THE ARCTIC

SEA MONSTERS

PENGUINS AND ANTARCTICA

LEONARDO DA VINCI

GHOSTS

LEPRECHAUNS AND IRISH FOLKLORE

RAGS AND RICHES: KIDS IN THE TIME OF
CHARLES DICKENS

SNAKES AND OTHER REPTILES

DOG HEROES

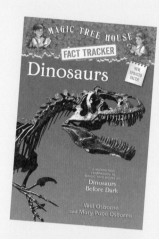

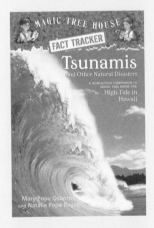

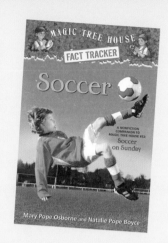

More Magic Tree House®

And coming soon:

**ANIMAL GAMES AND PUZZLES
FROM THE TREE HOUSE**

Mary Pope Osborne and **Natalie Pope Boyce** are sisters who grew up on army posts all over the world. They work together on Magic Tree House® Fact Tracker books to give readers information about the places, time periods, and animals that Jack and Annie discover in their Magic Tree House adventures.

Mary lives in northwest Connecticut. Natalie makes her home nearby in the Berkshire Hills of Massachusetts. Mary is the author of all the Magic Tree House® fiction titles, as well as many more books for kids.